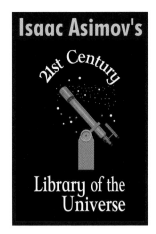

Isaac Asimov's

21st Century

Library of the
Universe

Fact and Fantasy

Legends, Folklore, and Outer Space

BY ISAAC ASIMOV

WITH REVISIONS AND UPDATING BY RICHARD HANTULA

Gareth Stevens Publishing
A WORLD ALMANAC EDUCATION GROUP COMPANY

Please visit our web site at: www.garethstevens.com
For a free color catalog describing Gareth Stevens Publishing's list of high-quality books
and multimedia programs, call 1-800-542-2595 (USA) or 1-800-387-3178 (Canada).
Gareth Stevens Publishing's fax: (414) 332-3567.

Library of Congress Cataloging-in-Publication Data

Asimov, Isaac.
      Legends, folklore, and outer space / by Isaac Asimov; with revisions and updating by Richard Hantula.
            p. cm. — (Isaac Asimov's 21st century library of the universe. Fact and fantasy)
      Includes bibliographical references and index.
      ISBN 0-8368-3951-X (lib. bdg.)
      1. Astronomy—Folklore. 2. Astronomy—Juvenile literature. I. Hantula, Richard. II. Title.
      QB46.A783   2004
      523.1—dc22   2004048170

This edition first published in 2005 by
Gareth Stevens Publishing
A World Almanac Education Group Company
330 West Olive Street, Suite 100
Milwaukee, WI 53212 USA

Series editor: Betsy Rasmussen
Cover design and layout adaptation: Melissa Valuch
Picture research: Matthew Groshek
Additional picture research: Diane Laska-Swanke
Production director: Jessica Morris
Production assistant: Nicole Esko

The editors at Gareth Stevens Publishing have selected science author Richard Hantula to bring
this classic series of young people's information books up to date. Richard Hantula has written
and edited books and articles on science and technology for more than two decades. He was
the senior U.S. editor for the *Macmillan Encyclopedia of Science*.

In addition to Hantula's contribution to this most recent edition, the editors would like to
acknowledge the participation of two noted science authors, Greg Walz-Chojnacki and
Francis Reddy, as contributors to earlier editions of this work.

Printed in the United States of America

1 2 3 4 5 6 7 8 9 09 08 07 06 05 04

Contents

• Legends, Folklore, and Outer Space •

We live in an enormously large place – the Universe. It's only natural that we would want to understand this place, so scientists and engineers have developed instruments and spacecraft that have told us far more about the Universe than we could possibly imagine.

We have seen planets up close, and spacecraft have even landed on some. We have learned about quasars and pulsars, supernovas and colliding galaxies, and black holes and dark matter. We have gathered amazing data about how the Universe may have come into being and how it may end. Nothing could be more astonishing.

But in ancient times, people looked at the sky with only their eyes – and were awed by what they saw. They created stories that helped them make sense of what they observed in the sky. Many of these stories, now considered folklore and legends, influence our view of the Universe to this very day.

Sun Worship

The Sun gives us light and warmth. Near Earth's Equator, the Sun climbs high in the sky. But farther north or south, the Sun sometimes remains low in the sky. When this happens, the days become shorter and cooler, and winter comes. Winter is a reminder that, without the Sun, there would be only darkness and freezing cold. People in ancient times commonly pictured the Sun as a glorious and good god.

The ancient Greeks imagined that their Sun god, Helios, drove a flaming chariot across the sky. The Babylonians said that their Sun god, Shamash, provided laws for people to follow. The Egyptian Sun god, Ra, was considered the nation's protector. One king of Egypt, Akhenaton, thought the Sun god was the only god.

Right: A time-lapse photo of the Sun in the Arctic.

Does Sirius cause the "dog days" of summer?

The sky's brightest star (other than the Sun) is Sirius, which belongs to the constellation, or group of stars, called Canis Major (Great Dog). Sirius itself is known as the Dog Star. Ancient Greeks thought Sirius was so bright that it must deliver heat to Earth like a smaller Sun.

In midsummer, Sirius and our Sun both rose at about the same time, and it was believed that the combination of the two explained why it was so hot in that period of the year. This is not true, but we still call the hottest part of summer in the Northern Hemisphere the "dog days."

Throughout history people have had various images of the Sun: an image from Europe in the Middle Ages (*below, left*); a dragon below the fiery Sun from eighteenth-century China (*below, right*); and the great eye of Ra, Sun god of the ancient Egyptians (*above*).

Moon Cycles

The Moon is much less bright than the Sun. In ancient myths, it is often pictured as a gentle female. The Greeks called her Selene; the Romans called her Luna.

The Moon changes its appearance, going through a cycle from a thin crescent to a full moon and back to a thin crescent. Ancient calendars were based on this cycle, which takes about one month. Twelve of the cycles made up one year.

As a matter of fact, both the word *month* and the word *Monday* come from the word *moon*.

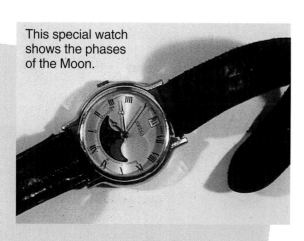

This special watch shows the phases of the Moon.

Above: For as long as people have gazed at the Moon, they have imagined pictures on its face. Look for the "man in the moon" (*top*), the "rabbit" (*center*), and the "maiden" (*bottom*).

Above: The ancient Greeks pictured the Moon as a beautiful maiden called Selene.

Right: This moon "monster" was drawn on the shield of a Crow Indian.

7

Wanderers of the Sky

From day to day and night to night, the Sun and Moon change their positions against the stars. The ancients saw five bright starlike objects, called planets, that also move across the sky. The word *planet* comes from the Greek word for "wanderer." Some ancient peoples named the planets after gods.

Our names for these five planets come from the ancient Romans.

The brightest planet in the sky is Venus, named for the goddess of love and beauty. A red planet the color of blood is Mars, named after the god of war. The fastest-moving planet is Mercury, named after the messenger of the gods. The slowest planet known in ancient times was Saturn, named for the god of agriculture. The second brightest planet in the sky, Jupiter, was named for the chief god. Jupiter is not as bright as Venus, but it shines all night; Venus appears only in the evening or at dawn.

Below: Ancient Chinese names for the four brightest planets.

Water Star – MERCURY

Fire Star – MARS

Gold Star – VENUS

Wood Star – JUPITER

Above: This ancient Babylonian view of the Universe shows a disk of land with water all around. Babylonia is shown at the center of the disk.

Was this an ancient observatory? A story in the Bible tells how the people of a Babylonian city tried to build a stairway to the stars – the Tower of Babel.

9

The "New" Planets

In modern times, scientists have discovered additional planets that are too far away from Earth to be seen without special instruments. These planets have been named after gods, too.

Beyond Saturn is Uranus, named for the ancient Greek god of the heavens. Then comes Neptune, a sea-green planet named for the Roman god of the sea. Beyond Neptune is Pluto, named for the Greek and Roman god of the underworld — because it is so far from the light of the Sun.

Many satellites, or moons, are also named for figures from mythology — the traditional stories about the gods. Neptune's largest satellite, Triton, is named after the son of the Greek god of the sea. Among other satellites with mythological names are Charon (Pluto's moon); Io and Leda (moons of Jupiter); and Atlas, Phoebe, and Prometheus (moons of Saturn).

Mythological names are often given to other objects in the Solar System as well, such as asteroids. The first asteroid to be found, in 1801, was named Ceres, after the Roman goddess of agriculture. Quaoar — a large object found in the Kuiper Belt beyond Neptune in 2002 — got its name from the mythology of California's Tongva Indian people. An even larger object was later found in an orbit going beyond the Kuiper Belt, and its discoverers proposed calling it Sedna, after the sea goddess of the Arctic Inuit people.

Name that planet!

Pluto, the ninth planet from the Sun, was discovered in 1930. Because it is so far from the Sun, it receives only dim light. For this reason, an eleven-year-old English girl suggested it be named after Pluto, the Greek and Roman god of the dark underworld. Also, "PL," the first letters of Pluto, are the initials of Percival Lowell, the man who built the observatory at which Pluto was first seen. Lowell in 1905 had launched the search for a planet beyond Neptune.

Left: Percival Lowell, the astronomer who began the search for a planet beyond Neptune.

Below: In ancient Greek mythology, Charon ferried the souls of the dead across the Styx River and into the underworld of Pluto. In 1978, when a moon was discovered orbiting the planet Pluto, the name Charon fit the new world perfectly.

Above: Pluto, god of the underworld, in the kingdom of death.

Left: According to Norse myths, at the end of the world, the Sun and Moon will each be swallowed by a giant wolf.

Above: In one Hindu story, the dragon Rahu causes an eclipse whenever he catches the Sun or Moon.

Creatures Hiding the Light

Every so often, something unusual happens in the sky — the Sun or Moon is eclipsed, or blocked from view. The Sun is eclipsed when the Moon moves in front of it and hides its light. The Moon is eclipsed when it moves into Earth's shadow.

Ancient peoples didn't know the scientific reasons for these occurrences, so they invented reasons of their own. Some thought the Sun and Moon were chased by wolves, dragons, or other creatures that caught up with them now and then and started to swallow them. People would shout and bang drums to scare the creatures away and bring back the Sun and Moon.

Of course, the Sun and Moon have always come back from their eclipses. And they continue to do so, even though, according to Norse myths, they will finally be swallowed by giant wolves.

During a lunar eclipse, the Moon's bright face turns a dusky red as it slips into Earth's shadow.

Meteorites — a big hit!

Now and then, a "shooting star" can be seen in the sky. Some people think shooting stars fall, but they are actually meteoroids that streak through Earth's atmosphere and become what are known as meteors. In some cases, they even strike Earth and are called meteorites. Ancient peoples thought meteorites were holy objects. In Mecca, Saudi Arabia, the building known as the Kaaba, which Muslims consider sacred, contains a Black Stone that may be a meteorite. But scientists are not allowed to study it, so nobody really knows for certain.

The Impending Doom of Comets

Comets are hazy objects with long tails. With a little imagination, they might look like a person's head with long, streaming hair. In fact, the word comet comes from the Greek word for "hair." At times, comets look like swords, so ancient peoples had reason to think of them as unpleasant omens. Most ancients thought comets were messages sent by the gods, warning of war, plague, and destruction. People would pray or ring church bells in order to try to ward off the evil.

But evil always came when there were comets in the sky. Of course, evil always came when comets were not in the sky, too — but people somehow didn't notice that!

Above: This drawing of the "Great War Comet" from 1861 bears a resemblance to Jefferson Davis, president of the Confederate States of America.

More bark than bite!

Comet tails contain poisonous gases, but the tails are so thin that the poison in them can't hurt anyone. In 1910, Earth was about to pass through the tail of Halley's Comet. Astronomers assured people there was no danger, but many people panicked anyway, thinking they would be poisoned and die. Some scoundrels sold phony pills that they said would prevent comet poisoning. Of course, that danger did not exist in the first place.

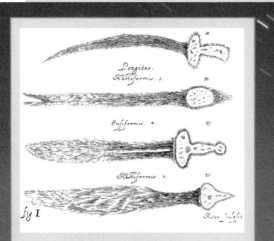

In earlier times, comets were often pictured as swordlike omens of war or disaster.

Comet Hale-Bopp loomed brightly in the sky in late 1996 and early 1997.

Constellations − Stars Together

When you look at the stars for a while, you'll find some that together form patterns. For instance, one group of stars in the northern sky can look like a *3*, an *E*, an *M*, or a *W*, depending on when you observe these stars. Ancient peoples associated star patterns with things that were familiar to them, such as tools, animals, gods, and their heroes.

Some of these patterns, mainly those developed by the Greeks and Romans, were recognized by astronomers as a handy way of dividing the sky into eighty-eight different areas. These areas are called constellations − a word that means "stars together."

Right: The constellation Taurus appears in the sky northwest of Orion. It is one of the oldest constellations mentioned in ancient historical accounts. It was seen as various animals and objects by different cultures.

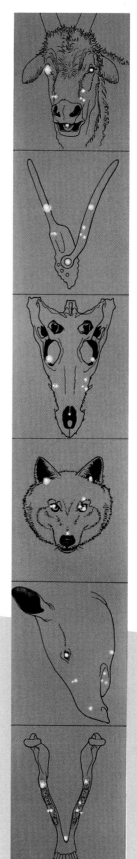

Bull
(Greek and Roman)

Nutcracker
(Indonesia)

Crocodile skull
(New Guinea)

Wolf
(Germany)

Tapir
(South America)

Bull's jaw
(Babylonia)

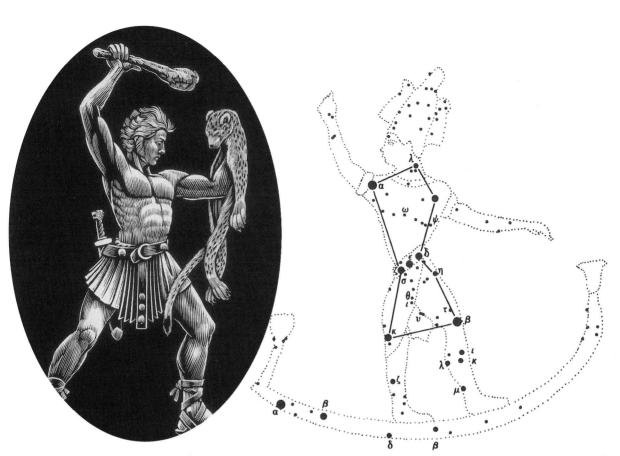

The constellation Orion is named for a great hunter in Greek mythology (*above*). But the constellation has been seen in different ways in various cultures. To the ancient Egyptians, it was Osiris, the God of the Underworld, sailing down the Nile River (*top, right*). For the Japanese, the two brightest stars of Orion each represented a warrior. Separated by the constellation's central three stars, the warriors are about to engage in combat (*bottom, left*). To the Bororo Indians of Brazil, Orion was Jabuti, the Turtle (*bottom, right*).

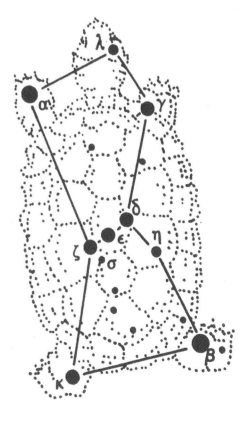

17

The Zodiac

It didn't take long for ancient peoples to realize that the Sun and Moon, along with the five planets they saw, never strayed from a single belt wrapped all the way around the sky. The ancients divided this belt into twelve constellations, which then became the twelve months of the lunar calendar. The Sun took one month to pass through each constellation. When the Sun had moved through all twelve constellations, a year had passed.

Top to bottom:
The rat, monkey, and rooster – three animals from the Japanese zodiac.

Most of these constellations were pictured as animals. So the band in which the Sun, Moon, and planets appeared to move became known as the "circle of animals" – or zodiac.

Some astronomers believe the zodiac was invented by the Babylonians of the Middle East about four thousand years ago and then made its way to Egypt, Greece, China, and eventually other countries and cultures.

Opposite: A thirteenth-century artist pictures the month of May. The Sun moves on a wagon driven by winged horses from the constellation Taurus (the Bull) into Gemini (the Twins).

19

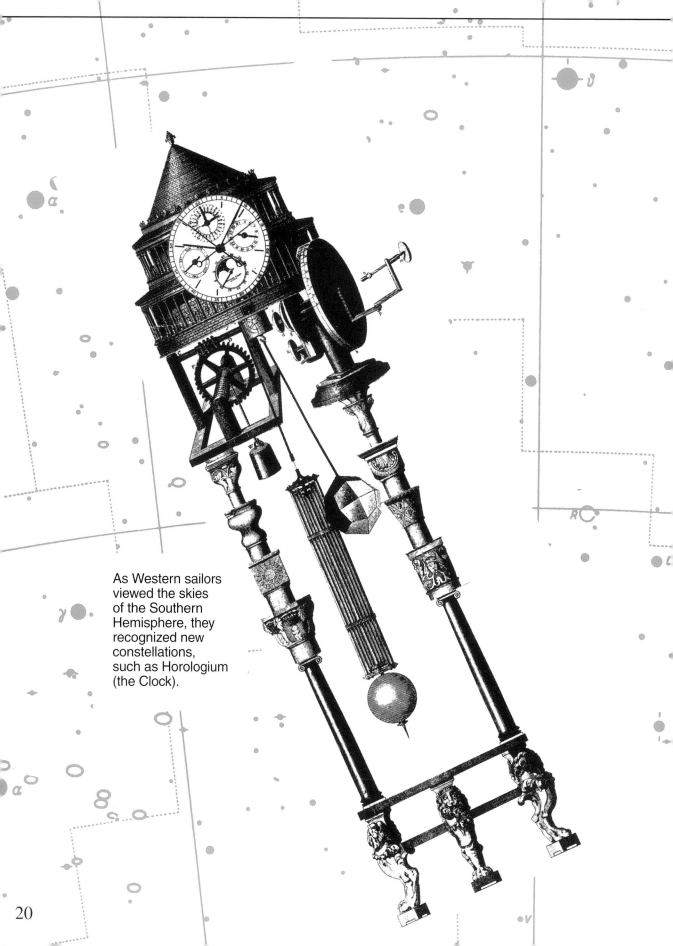

As Western sailors
viewed the skies
of the Southern
Hemisphere, they
recognized new
constellations,
such as Horologium
(the Clock).

The Southern Sky

Some constellations can be seen only from the Southern Hemisphere. As seafaring explorers from Europe sailed farther from their homelands, they found themselves looking at new and unfamiliar stars. Astronomers charted these new stars in detail in the seventeenth and eighteenth centuries. They recognized new constellations by "connecting the dots" – just as people had done for thousands of years. But the images used for these modern star patterns often seemed more technological than mythological. That's why the Southern Hemisphere has constellations such as Antlia (the Air Pump), Horologium (the Clock), Pyxis (the Compass), and Sextans (the Sextant).

Right: With the help of a device called a sextant and mathematical calculations, sailors could find their location on Earth by observing the positions of the Sun and stars.

Above: An artist's conception of our Galaxy, the Milky Way.

The Milky Way

Another part of the starry sky is the glow of our Galaxy, the Milky Way. The Milky Way contains billions of stars. From Earth, it looks like an irregular band of mist.

In ancient times, the Milky Way was often seen as a road, river, or bridge along which spirits of the dead left the land of the living. For some American Indians, the stars in the Milky Way were campfires where souls could rest on their long journey. The Babylonians and ancient Mongols viewed the Milky Way as a seam joining the two halves of heaven. They thought light from the palaces of the gods could be seen through tiny holes in the stitching.

The Inca people of Peru saw constellations within the band of the Milky Way. In some parts of the band, dark clouds of dust block the Milky Way's light from reaching Earth. These became "dark constellations," such as the Fox, the Llama, and the Snake.

The Inca people of Peru saw various constellations in the Milky Way's dark stretches of dust.

Polaris — the North Star

In the Northern Hemisphere, travelers have been guided for thousands of years by the star known as Polaris. Polaris is sometimes called the North Star because it shows where the direction North is located. It lies very near the spot on the sky toward which Earth's axis points. (The axis is the imaginary line around which Earth rotates.)

For people in Europe, North America, and northern Asia, the constellations closest to Polaris never set. The group of stars known as the Big Dipper, for example, seems to just spin around the sky. It changes positions throughout the night and over the year, but it's always above the horizon. For this reason, the Norse and the Mongols imagined Polaris as a spike which the heavens whirled around. The Chinese thought of it as an emperor, a chief star that ruled the others.

Polaris won't always be the North Star, nor has it always been. Earth's axis slowly wobbles, and over the coming centuries it will gradually point to different parts of the sky.

Left: The Big Dipper is one of the best-known star patterns. The Aztecs of Mexico saw their troublesome god Tezcatlipoca in the stars of the Big Dipper. Legend has it that another god was fed up with the problems Tezcatlipoca caused. This god turned Tezcatlipoca into a puppet and placed him in the sky, where he was forced to dance endlessly around Polaris.

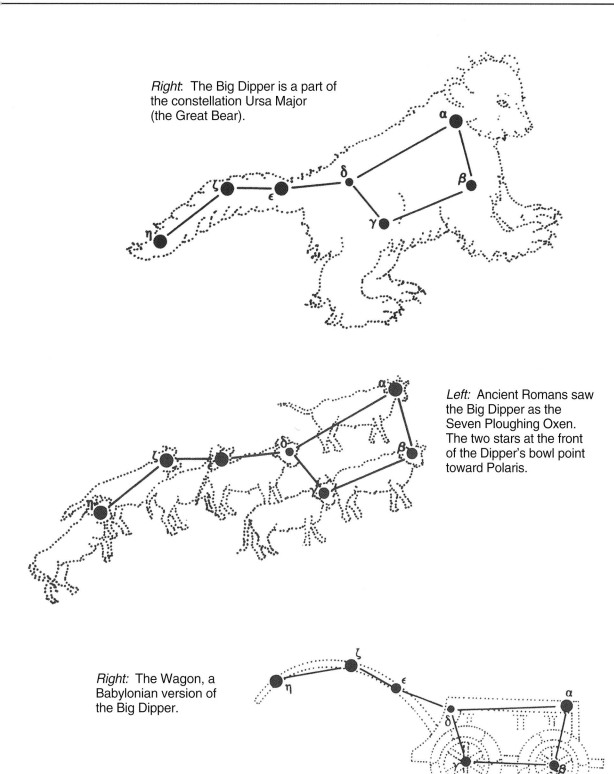

Right. The Big Dipper is a part of the constellation Ursa Major (the Great Bear).

Left: Ancient Romans saw the Big Dipper as the Seven Ploughing Oxen. The two stars at the front of the Dipper's bowl point toward Polaris.

Right: The Wagon, a Babylonian version of the Big Dipper.

25

Endless Exploration

As you can see, people tell stories about the objects in the sky in different ways. Astronomers talk about the skies in scientific ways. People known as astrologers try to predict the future by using the positions of the planets in the zodiac. This practice is called astrology. Scientists are skeptical about astrology, but many people believe it to be true, just as ancient peoples thought their stories of the skies to be true.

History shows that while secrets of the Universe are still being uncovered, one thing remains certain – our endless desire to explore and make sense of the skies above us.

Left: Astrologers have claimed throughout time that stars and planets influence our moods and fortunes. Even today, many major newspapers carry a horoscope for those who seek advice from the stars.

The demon star – look only if you dare!

Perseus, a hero in Greek mythology, killed Medusa, an evil being with snakes in her hair. Legend has it that people turned to stone when they looked at her. The constellation Perseus appears to hold the head of Medusa. One bright star stands out in her "head." It brightens and dims. The ancients called it the Demon Star. The Arabs named it Algol (the Ghoul), which is its name today.

An example of a
horoscope from a
recent year.

Horoscope

**Find your birthdate, and get
some advice from the stars!**

Aquarius

Birthdate: January 20 — February 19
Look for and talk with those
who share your interests.
Some great insights will
be revealed to you.

Pisces

Birthdate: February 20 — March 20
Be suspicious of people who
appear to share your interests.
They may be trying to take
advantage of you.

Aries

Birthdate: March 21 — April 19
Don't be discouraged by
mistakes you make today.
With a little patience,
everything will work out fine.

Taurus

Birthdate: April 20 — May 20
Listen to people carefully
today. Their advice could
be quite valuable.

Gemini

Birthdate: May 21 — June 20
People may say nice things
about you today. They may
want something from you.

Cancer

Birthdate: June 21 — July 22
Make plans for a long
automobile trip.

Leo

Birthdate: July 23 — August 22
Money could be available for
you to start your own business.

Virgo

Birthdate: August 23 — September 22
Someone may give you a
chance to spend a sizable sum
of money today. Be cautious
and think it over before taking
the plunge.

Libra

Birthdate: September 23 — October 23
There are people less fortunate
than you. Today, you will know
where to find them. Do what
you can for them.

Scorpio

Birthdate: October 24 — November 22
A good day to be with friends.
Find as many as you can with
birthdays close to yours and
celebrate together.

Sagittarius

Birthdate: November 23 — December 21
Don't confuse people by
rushing around. It is a good
stay-at-home day. Bake
something sweet.

Capricorn

Birthdate: December 22 — January 19
Be on the move today. Don't
stay in one place for long.
Keep people guessing.

Fact File: The Changing Sky

Sometimes it is hard to imagine what ancient stargazers had in mind when they gave names to groups of stars in the sky. For example, did the Greeks really see the figure of the mythological hunter Orion in a star pattern that can look more like the figure of an hourglass?

The fact is that people name things for many reasons. If a group of stars looks like a telescope, it might be named after a telescope. But sometimes it might be given a name from folklore or legend or might be named in honor of certain events or people. After all, areas of land on Earth are named for similar reasons. It would be unusual if a city or state named Washington actually looked like a profile of President George Washington.

There are also many reasons why the names, shapes, and legends of certain constellations may vanish. Sometimes, over the course of centuries, stars' positions in the sky shift enough to form new patterns. Sometimes a rich and thriving culture is conquered or disappears, and its constellation names are lost. Perhaps later generations simply choose to ignore a name that seems too sentimental. Or maybe a constellation does not disappear but is merely renamed.

None of the constellation names in the illustrations on these two pages or in the chart at right is used any longer to describe our ever-changing sky.

Above, left, and opposite:
Three constellations that have vanished:
Bufo (the Toad), Aranea (the Spider), and
the Archangel Gabriel.

Some Constellations of the Past

NAME	COMMENTS
Tiamat	Named by the Babylonians for a sea monster representing chaos who was killed by the hero god Marduk. The constellation Tiamat was "borrowed" from the Babylonians by the ancient Greeks. Today, it is known as Cetus (the Whale). According to Greek mythology, the Greek hero Perseus (another constellation) killed the monster Cetus in order to rescue the princess Andromeda (also one of the constellations).
Mons Maenalus	Named in the late seventeenth century for the mountain home of the Greek god Pan.
Bufo (the Toad)	Named in the mid-eighteenth century by John Hill, an eccentric English physician. It is composed of a noticeable cluster of stars near the constellations Scorpio and Libra.
Limax (the Slug)	Also named in the mid-eighteenth century by John Hill. The constellation represents a snail without its shell. Most of the stars in this constellation are toward the head and lower parts of the body, with few in the middle.
Felis (the Cat)	Named around 1800 by J. J. Le Francais de Lalande, a French astronomer who loved cats. The name has not been used since the nineteenth century.
Officina Typographica (the Printing Office)	Named in the late eighteenth century by the German astronomer Johann Bode to honor the invention of the printing press.
Telescopium Herschelii (Herschel's Telescope)	Named in 1781 by the Austrian astronomer Maximilian Hell to honor William Herschel, a German-born English astronomer who discovered Uranus in that year.
Circle of Chiefs	Named by the Skidi Pawnee Indians, who arranged their villages in patterns reflecting the positions of important star gods in the sky. Some authorities think this constellation, which represents Tirawahat, the Universe's central force, is our Corona Borealis (the Northern Crown).
Seven Boys Transformed into Geese	Named by the Chumash Indians of California. This constellation is the star pattern now called the Big Dipper.

More Books about Legends, Folklore, and Outer Space

The Book of Constellations: Discover the Secrets in the Stars. Robin Kerrod (Barrons)

Find the Constellations. H. A. Rey (Houghton Mifflin)

The New Patterns in the Sky: Myths and Legends of the Stars. Julius D. W. Staal (McDonald & Woodward)

The Starlore Handbook: An Essential Guide to the Night Sky. Geoffrey Cornelius (Chronicle)

Stars: A Golden Guide. Robert H. Baker and Herbert S. Zim (St. Martin's Press)

A Walk Through the Heavens: A Guide to Stars and Constellations and Their Legends. Milton D. Heifetz and Wil Tirion (Cambridge University Press)

DVDs

Atlas of the Sky. (Space Holdings)

The Standard Deviants: Astronomy Adventure. (Cerebellum)

Web Sites

The Internet sites listed here can help you learn more about the objects in the sky and the folklore, legends, and history connected with them.

Ancient Astronomy. www.astronomy.pomona.edu/archeo/
The Constellations. www.dibonsmith.com/
The Constellations and their Stars. www.astro.wisc.edu/~dolan/constellations/
Starlore. ching.apana.org.au/~paulc/
Students for the Exploration and Development of Space (SEDS). www.seds.org/
Windows to the Universe.
www.windows.ucar.edu/tour/link=/the_universe/uts/ast_history.html

Places to Visit

Here are some museums and centers where you can find exhibits about the Solar System, the stars and constellations, and other aspects of astronomy.

**Adler Planetarium and
 Astronomy Museum**
1300 S. Lake Shore Drive
Chicago, Illinois 60605

American Museum of Natural History
Rose Center for Earth and Space
Central Park West at 79th Street
New York, NY 10024

National Air and Space Museum
Smithsonian Institution
6th and Independence Avenue SW
Washington, DC 20560

Odyssium
11211 142nd Street
Edmonton, Alberta T5M4A1
Canada

Scienceworks Museum
2 Booker Street
Spotswood, Victoria 3015
Australia

StarDome Observatory
One Tree Hill Domain, off Manukau Road
Royal Oak, Auckland
New Zealand

Glossary

asteroids: very small "planets." More than a million of them exist in our Solar System. Most of them orbit the Sun between Mars and Jupiter, but many are found elsewhere.

astrology: the study of the positions of the stars and planets and their supposed influence upon humans and events on Earth.

astronomer: a person involved in the scientific study of the Universe and its various bodies.

calendar: a system for dividing time, most commonly into days, weeks, and months. Every calendar has a starting day and ending day for the year.

comet: an object in space made of ice, rock, and dust. When its orbit brings it closer to the Sun, it develops a tail of gas and dust.

constellation: a grouping of stars in the sky that seems to trace a familiar figure or symbol. Constellations are named after something they are thought to resemble.

"dog days": the period between early July and early September when the hot weather of summer usually occurs in the Northern Hemisphere.

eclipse: the partial or complete blocking of light from one astronomical body by another.

galaxy: a large star system containing up to hundreds of billions of stars, along with gas and dust.

Halley's Comet: a comet, named for English astronomer Edmond Halley, that passes by Earth once every 76 years or so. Its first recorded sighting was around 240 B.C. Its most recent pass occurred in 1986.

Kuiper Belt: bodies that are smaller than planet size and lie in the region of the Solar System starting just beyond Neptune's orbit.

meteor: a meteoroid that has entered Earth's atmosphere. Also, the bright streak of light made as the meteoroid enters or moves through the atmosphere. If the meteoroid lands on Earth, it is called a meteorite.

meteoroid: a lump of rock or metal drifting through space. Meteoroids can be as big as small asteroids or as small as specks of dust.

Milky Way: the glowing mist of stars in the sky that is our Galaxy.

mythology: the traditional stories, or "myths," about the gods and legendary heroes of a group of people.

planet: one of the large bodies that revolve around a star like our Sun.

satellite: a small body in space that moves in an orbit around a larger body.

Solar System: the Sun with the planets and all the other bodies, such as asteroids, that orbit the Sun.

underworld: in the mythology of some peoples, the place where people are thought to go when they die.

zodiac: the band of constellations across the sky that represents the paths of the Sun, the Moon, and all the planets except Pluto.

Index

Born in 1920, Isaac Asimov came to the United States as a young boy from his native Russia. As a young man, he was a student of biochemistry. In time, he became one of the most productive writers the world has ever known. His books cover a spectrum of topics, including science, history, language theory, fantasy, and science fiction. His brilliant imagination gained him the respect and admiration of adults and children alike. Sadly, Isaac Asimov died shortly after the publication of the first edition of *Isaac Asimov's Library of the Universe.*

The publishers wish to thank the following for permission to reproduce copyright and other material: front cover, 3, © Andrew C. Stewart/Fortean Picture Library; 4 (upper), 6 (upper left), 8 (upper), 13 (upper), 14 (upper), 16 (left), 18 (upper), 24 (upper), 28 (upper left), (postage stamps), from the collection of George G. Young, Astronomy Study Unit of the American Topical Association; 4 (lower), © Forrest Baldwin; 5 (upper and lower right), 7 (upper), Michael Holford; 5 (lower left), copyright-free reproduction from Ridley's *A Short Treatise of Magnetic Bodies and Motions*; 6 (lower left), 26, Matthew Groshek/© Gareth Stevens, Inc., 1989; 6 (right, all), 12 (both), 17 (lower left), Rick Karpinski/DeWalt and Associates, 1989; 7 (lower), copyright-free reproduction of a Crow Indian shield; 9 (upper), 11 (lower right), 21, Mary Evans Picture Library; 9 (lower), Kunsthistorisches Museum; 11 (upper), Lowell Observatory; 11 (lower left), © Keith Ward 1989; 13 (lower), © Matthew Groshek 1986; 14 (lower), Historical Pictures Service, Chicago; 15 (large), © Kevin and Betty Collins/Visuals Unlimited; 15 (inset), 28 (upper right and lower left), 29, Adler Planetarium, Chicago; 16 (right, all), © Sally Bensusen 1989; 17 (upper and lower right), 24 (lower), 25 (all), Julius D. W. Staal, 1988. *The New Patterns in the Sky: Myths and Legends of the Stars*. The McDonald & Woodward Publishing Company, Blacksburg, Virginia; 18 (lower, all), © Matthew Powell, 1989; 19, Giraudon/Art Resource, New York; 20, © Gareth Stevens, Inc., 1989; 22, © Chris Butler/Astrostock; 23, © Sally Bensusen.